Collins Easy Learning

Handwriting Workbook 2

Age 7-9

Karina Law

This book belongs to

How to use this book

- Easy Learning workbooks help your child improve basic skills, build confidence and develop a love of learning.

- Find a quiet, comfortable place to work, away from distractions.

- Get into a routine of completing one or two workbook pages with your child every day.

- Ask your child to circle the star that matches how many activities they have completed every two pages:

Some = half of the activities   Most = more than half   All = all the activities

- The progress certificate at the back of this book will help you and your child keep track of how many ⭐ have been circled.

- Encourage your child to work through all of the activities eventually, and praise them for completing the progress certificate.

- Each workbook builds on the previous one in the series. Help your child complete this one to ensure they have covered what they need to know before starting the next workbook.

- Help your child to rest their pencil in the 'V' between their thumb and index finger; their fingers should be between one and two centimetres away from the pencil tip.

- Introduce your child to the 'starting point' in each activity, where they should first place their pencil or pen on the paper.

- You may find that it helps your child to say aloud the patterns and words as they write.

Parent tip
Look out for tips on how to help your child with handwriting practice.

- Ask your child to find and colour the little monkeys that are hidden throughout this book.

- This will help engage them with the pages of the book and get them interested in the activities.

(Don't count this one.)

Published by Collins
An imprint of HarperCollins*Publishers*
77–85 Fulham Palace Road
Hammersmith
London
W6 8JB

Browse the complete Collins catalogue at
www.collinseducation.com

First published in 2011
© HarperCollins*Publishers* 2011

10 9 8 7 6 5 4 3 2

ISBN-13 978-0-00-727759-9

The author asserts the moral right to be identified as the author of this work.

British Library Cataloguing in Publication Data
A catalogue record for this publication is available from the British Library

Written by Karina Law
Based on content by Sue Peet
Design, layout and cover design by Linda Miles, Lodestone Publishing
Illustrated by Peter Bull Art Studio, Graham Smith, Andy Tudor and Jenny Tulip
Cover illustration by Andy Tudor and Jenny Tulip
Packaged and project managed by White-Thomson Publishing Ltd
Printed and bound by Martins the Printers, Berwick Upon Tweed

Contents

Alphabet practice

Parent tip
Help your child to think of and write another food word for each letter of the alphabet.

1 Read the words below. Some of them have already been put into alphabetical order. Write out the missing words.

> honey   rice   spaghetti   muffin   apple
> lemon   bread   waffle   vegetables
> orange   kiwi fruit   grapes   cake   yoghurt
> fish   ugli fruit   quiche   nuts
> zucchini   doughnut   pizza   toast   jelly
> ice cream   eggs   box of chocolates

a _____

b _____

c _____

doughnut _____

e _____

f _____

g _____

h _____

i _____

j _____

kiwi fruit _____

l _____

2 Write the food words from the box on page 4 next to the correct letter.

_m_ _____

_n_ _____

_o_ _____

_p_ _____

_q_ _____

_r_ _____

_s_ _____

_t_ _____

_u_ _____

_v_ _____

_w_ _____

box of chocolates _____

_y_ _____

zucchini _____

Digraphs: wh, ph

1 Read the wh words. Then write each one three times.

whistle

whisper

whiskers

wheat

wheelchair

whale

whirlwind

2 Read the ph words. Then write each one three times.

paragraph

trophy

telephone

phonics

sphere

Parent tip
When reading books with your child, ask them to point out words beginning with **wh** and **ph**.

3 Read each question word. Then write it out three times.

what _____

where _____

why _____

which _____

4 Read the jokes and copy the punchlines.

Where do you weigh whales?

In a whale weigh station!

What do you call an elephant that never washes?

A smellyphant!

Prefixes: re, pre

1 Read these words beginning with re. Then write each one three times.

repair _____

reflect _____

remember _____

repeat _____

reassure _____

reform _____

recreate _____

2 Read these words beginning with pre. Then write each one three times.

prepare _____

pretend _____

prehistoric _____

prevent _____

predict _____

Parent tip
Look for more words beginning with **re** and **pre** in a dictionary, then call them out and ask your child to write them down.

Word endings: tion

3 Trace the dotted letters. Then write them out three times.

tion *tion* _____

4 Read these words ending in tion. Then write each one three times.

information _____

fiction _____

instruction _____

competition _____

addition _____

action _____

attention _____

station _____

subtraction _____

imagination _____

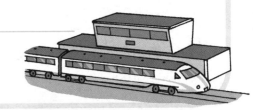

How much did you do?   Activities 1–4

Circle the star
to show what
you have done.

 Some

 Most

 All

School rules

These school rules are muddled up. Draw a line to join the start of the sentence to the correct ending. Then write out the correct rules neatly on the opposite page.

Do not talk   to yourself.

Do not drop litter   without your teacher's permission.

Do not run   in the playground.

Do not chew gum   during Assembly.

Keep your hands and feet   in class.

Do not leave the classroom   tidy.

Keep your belongings   in the corridors.

School Rules

1 _____

2 _____

3 _____

4 _____

5 _____

6 _____

7 _____

Parent tip
Help your child make and decorate their own notebook for handwriting practice.

How much did you do?   Activities 1-2

Circle the star to show what you have done.

Some

Most

All

Spelling patterns: oy, oi, ar

1 Read each word. Then write it out three times.

enjoy _____

employ _____

annoy _____

boil _____

noisy _____

disappoint _____

2 Read each word. Then write it out three times.

alarm _____

artist _____

market _____

shark _____

3 Read and write.

The noisy alarm was very annoying.

_____

_____

Compound words

4 A compound word is made up of two other words. Join up the words to make compound words. Then write each one out twice.

milk — corn   milkshake _____

fire — shake   _____

pop   room   _____

class   work   _____

life   berry   _____

green   boat   _____

super   way   _____

straw   house   _____

gold   site   _____

motor   market   _____

web   fish   _____

Parent tip
Make up rhymes for your child to write down.

How much did you do?   Activities 1–4

Circle the star to show what you have done.

 Some   Most   All

Idioms

1 An idiom is a saying. Read and copy these idioms. Do you know what they mean?

Pull your socks up!

Don't put all your eggs in one basket.

Parent tip
Help your child find more idioms from a book or the Internet to copy out.

Keep your hair on.

Don't let the cat out of the bag.

Now you've put your foot in it!

Don't count your chickens before they hatch.

2 Choose a word to complete each saying. Then write the whole sentence.

> fly dogs bell cat cake book

It's raining cats and _____.

_____

A piece of _____.

_____

Saved by the _____.

_____

Pigs might _____!

_____

You can't judge a _____ by its cover.

_____

Curiosity killed the _____.

_____

Suffixes: ful, ly

1 Read these words ending with ful. Then write each one three times.

peaceful _____

careful _____

beautiful _____

spoonful _____

painful _____

playful _____

Parent tip
Use the progress certificate at the back of this book to make a reward chart for your child.

2 Look again at the words above. Now choose the correct word to complete each sentence.

A _____ of porridge.

A _____ experience.

Be _____ !

A _____ night's sleep.

A _____ flower.

A _____ puppy.

3 Look at the words below. Add ful or ly to each word. Then write out the whole word.

help _____   forget _____   quick _____

helpful _____   _____   _____

wonder _____   excited _____   slow _____

_____   _____   _____

hope _____   wise _____   sudden _____

_____   _____   _____

silent _____   thought _____   quiet _____

_____   _____   _____

cold _____   kind _____   truth _____

_____   _____   _____

How much did you do?   ## Activities 1–3

Circle the star to show what you have done.

 Some   Most   All

Similes

We use similes to compare one thing with another. They usually begin with 'as' or 'like'. Draw a line to join the start of each simile to the correct ending.

Parent tip
Find other well-known similes and ask your child to write them down.

As proud as a   lamb

As gentle as a   flash

As white as   pie

As stubborn as a   peacock

As cool as a   owl

As dry as a   fiddle

As easy as   snow

As fit as a   cucumber

As wise as an   bone

As quick as a   mule

2 Look again at the similes opposite that you have joined. Write each one in your best handwriting.

(blank lined writing space)

3 Complete these two similes in your own words.

My heart is beating like _____

The full moon shines like _____

Words within words

Look at the words below. Write each one out three times. Find a smaller word inside each one and underline it. Then write out the smaller word three times.

witch   <u>witch</u>   <u>witch</u>

<u>itch</u>   itch   itch

Parent tip
Look for words within words on items around the house such as food packets.

history

monkey

cupboard

balloon

garage

heart

danger

20

2 Look at the words below. Write each one out three times. Find a smaller word inside each one and underline it. Then write out the smaller word three times.

fairy _____

_____

chocolate _____

_____

tomato _____

_____

carrot _____

_____

glove _____

_____

pyjamas _____

_____

elephant _____

_____

minute _____

_____

How much did you do?   Activities 1–2

Circle the star
to show what
you have done.   ★

                        Some   Most   All

Shape poem: 'Kite'

1   This poem 'Kite' works well as a shape poem. The words have been set out in the shape of a kite. Read the poem.

A
kite
on the
ground is
just paper and
string but up in the
air it will dance and sing.
A kite in the air will
dance and will caper
but back on the
ground is just
string and
paper.

2 Copy the poem in the kite shape below in your best handwriting.

Parent tip
Read the poem out loud with your child when they have copied it out.

How much did you do?   Activities 1–2

Circle the star
to show what
you have done.   Some   Most   All

23

Riddles

1 A riddle is a word puzzle. The words in the box below are the answers to some riddles. Copy the riddles. Then choose the correct answer from the words in the box. Write the answer.

A cold. A comb. A hole. Light. A staircase.

What gets bigger the more you take away?

_____

_____

What goes up and down but does not move?

_____

_____

What can fill a room but takes up no space?

_____

_____

What can you catch but not throw?

_____

_____

What has teeth but won't bite?

_____

_____

Handwriting practice: 'A cheerful old bear at the zoo'

2 Write this poem in your best handwriting.

A cheerful old bear at the zoo
Could always find something to do.
When it bored him to go
On a walk to and fro
He reversed it, and walked fro and to.

Lewis Carroll

How much did you do?   Activities 1-2

Circle the star to show what you have done.

 Some

 Most

 All

Proverbs

1 A proverb is a popular saying that teaches a lesson about life. Read the proverb. Then write it in your best handwriting.

Early to bed and early to rise,
Makes a man healthy, wealthy and wise.

_____

_____

_____

_____

2 Read the proverb. Then write it in your best handwriting.

Too many cooks spoil the broth.

_____

_____

3 Read the proverb. Then write it in your best handwriting.

After dinner, sit awhile.
After supper, walk a mile.

_____

_____

_____

_____

4 Read the proverb. Then write it in your best handwriting.

An apple a day keeps the doctor away.

_____

_____

5 Read the proverb. Then write it in your best handwriting.

The early bird catches the worm.

_____

_____

6 Read the proverb. Then write it in your best handwriting.

A stitch in time saves nine.

_____

_____

Parent tip
Write out other proverbs on a piece of paper, with spaces for some of the words. Then ask your child to fill in the missing words.

7 Read the proverb. Then write it in your best handwriting.

Two wrongs don't make a right.

_____

_____

How much did you do?   Activities 1–7

Circle the star to show what you have done.

 Some

 Most

 All

Capital letters

1 Capital letters don't join on to any other letters.
Trace and write. Start at the green dot.

A A A B B B C C C

D D D E E E F F F

G G G H H H I I I

J J J K K K L L L

M M M N N N O O O

P P P Q Q Q R R R

S S S T T T U U U

V V V W W W X X X

Y Y Y Z Z Z

Around the world

Write a label on each country. Begin each name with a capital letter. Use an atlas if you need to.

France   Spain   Germany   Italy

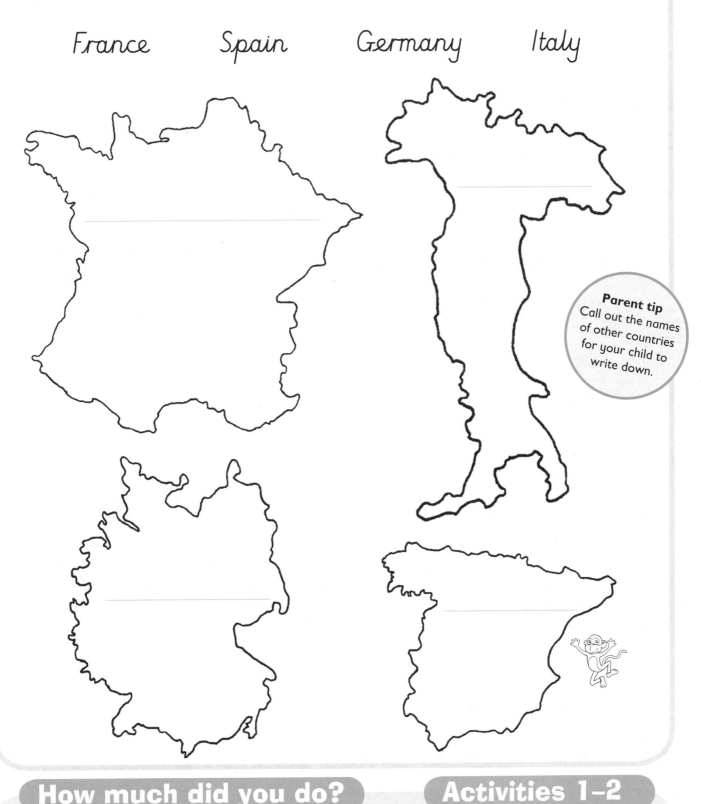

Parent tip
Call out the names of other countries for your child to write down.

How much did you do?   Activities 1–2

Circle the star to show what you have done.

 Some   Most   All

Book titles

1 Choose the correct book title to write on each book.
Remember to use capital letters.

The Haunted House by Hugo First

Love and Marriage by Annie Versary

How to Make Money by Jack Pott

Climate Change by Gail Force

Astronomy by I. C. Stars

Bird Watching by Jack Daw

Recycling by D. Sposable

_____

_____

_____

I. C. Stars

_____

_____

_____

Gail Force

_____

_____

_____

Jack Daw

Parent tip
Ask your child
to copy the titles
and authors of
books on their
bookshelf.

2 Choose the correct book title to write on each book.
Remember to use capital letters.

_____

_____

_____

Hugo First

_____

_____

_____

Jack Pott

_____

_____

_____

D. Sposable

_____

_____

_____

Annie Versary

How much did you do?   **Activities 1–2**

Circle the star
to show what
you have done.   Some   Most   All

31

Check your progress

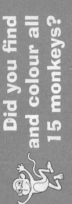

Did you find and colour all 15 monkeys?

(Including this one!)

- Shade in the stars on the progress certificate to show how much you did. Shade one star for every ⭐ you circled in this book.
- If you have shaded fewer than 10 stars go back to the pages where you circled Some ⭐ or Most ⭐ and try those pages again.
- If you have shaded 10 or more stars you are ready to move on to the next workbook. Well done!

Collins Easy Learning Handwriting Age 7–9 Workbook 2

Progress certificate

name _____

to

date _____

Alphabet practice	Digraphs: wh, ph	Prefixes: re, pre Word endings: tion	School rules	Spelling patterns: oy, oi, ar Compound words	Idioms	Suffixes: ful, ly	Similes	Words within words	Shape poem	Riddles Hand-writing practice	Proverbs	Capital letters Around the world	Book titles
pages 4–5	pages 6–7	pages 8–9	pages 10–11	pages 12–13	pages 14–15	pages 16–17	pages 18–19	pages 20–21	pages 22–23	pages 24–25	pages 26–27	pages 28–29	pages 30–31
☆ 1	☆ 2	☆ 3	☆ 4	☆ 5	☆ 6	☆ 7	☆ 8	☆ 9	☆ 10	☆ 11	☆ 12	☆ 13	☆ 14